How to Build a More Effective Board

By THOMAS P. HOLLAND

The performance of governing boards of nonprofit organizations is receiving increasing attention, both from outside critics and from concerned board members themselves. While many call for boards to improve their effectiveness, few have much confidence about what to do to accomplish that goal. Suggestions abound regarding board size and composition, meeting frequency and duration, committee structures, and such. Others wonder whether a stronger board would do more than just meddle more extensively in administrative matters.

Many books offer advice on improving board performance. However, few are based on any systematic research, and few provide evidence that boards actually improved their performance based on the advice offered.

Not only is it difficult to gauge improvements in board performance, but assessing the quality of board decisions and monitoring their consequences for the organization is also difficult. This is the case because often board members' roles and performance expectations are ill-defined. Most boards have little objective evidence of the value they add to their organizations, and board accountability is ambiguous. Possibly because of its inherent ambiguity, efforts to improve board performance find little enthusiasm among some board members.

However, if methods of enhancing board effectiveness and performance were less ambiguous, boards could not only learn from their successful counterparts, but confidently strive to improve their effectiveness using proven methods.

With this possibility in mind, fellow researchers Richard Chait, Barbara Taylor, and I spent several years of intensive study trying to determine why some nonprofit boards excel while others falter. In the course of our research we interviewed several hundred board members and chief executives and surveyed more than 1,000 others. Six characteristics emerged that distinguish high-performing boards from their less successful counterparts. Identifying and quantifying these competencies (a specific discussion of the competencies and the characteristics of each can be found on pages 6 and 7 and a full discussion is contained in our book, *The Effective Board of Trustees*) caused us to take the question one step further: If characteristics of effective boards are discernible, is it then possible for boards to improve their performance through intentional change? This question is the topic of our second book, *Improving the Performance of Governing Boards* published by Oryx Press, as well as this booklet.

2

Lessons Learned

The skills and practices of high-performing boards serve as examples for other boards to consider. While not every practice may be transferable, boards that want to improve their effectiveness can draw selectively upon the lessons offered by their high-performing counterparts and adapt them locally.

Our interviews, coaching, and observations of boards over these several years identified a number of important lessons regarding how boards can work on improving their performance. (These lessons are discussed more fully in our book *Improving the Performance of Governing Boards.*) The research helped us identify situations that may stimulate boards to examine their performance, conditions necessary for board development to succeed, ways to assess current performance, and practical suggestions for restructuring how boards conduct their business to ensure peak performance.

CONDITIONS FOR SUCCESSFUL BOARD DEVELOPMENT

Ambiguous expectations of boards, weak accountability, unclear returns on the investments of time for development, and discomforts over giving up familiar patterns and practicing new ones all serve as obstacles to improving board performance. Overcoming these barriers requires the board's concerted and sustained attention. For these efforts to be successful, several prerequisites must be in place.

Board development cannot be imposed on board members or the chief executive. In order for improvement to take place, a board must be ready for change and accept the importance of attending to and improving its own performance. The chief executive, the board chairperson, and a substantial number of board leaders must want to work on improving board performance. These leaders must initiate the process with enthusiasm and clear commitment to working with the board to bring about changes.

Efforts to improve performance must be integrated with the board's regular business. Learning to work together more effectively cannot be accomplished in a one-time session or retreat—learning must be embedded in the board's regular work. By looking at the board's tasks and identifying ways the group can work better and produce more useful results, the board simultaneously learns and applies its new techniques. While a retreat approach is often useful in getting started, development activities should be built into the board's ongoing agenda and ways of doing business. Most board members are motivated to improve the way the board functions primarily so that the board is better equipped to enhance the organization's performance. Board development framed as a means to improve overall organizational performance, rather than merely the performance of the board, is often met with greater enthusiasm.

Changing a board's behavior is easier than changing attitudes or personalities. Exhortations and prescriptions do not work nearly as well as changes in routines, procedures, or structures for doing work together. Board members begin to think differently and act differently as a result of such practical steps as bringing thoughtful questions to the board, providing relevant and focused information, dividing members into small groups to brainstorm alternative solutions and formulate recommendations, and encouraging critical and analytical thinking about issues before the group.

The best approaches link process and substance. For example, asking the board to set goals for itself or to formulate indicators to monitor its performance sets in motion a process that builds cohesion and educates participants, while also generating substantive products.

Board development is an extensive, long-term process, not a quick-fix. The effort to improve board performance is never complete. In order to sustain the process, the board needs members who serve as champions. The pressures to revert to business as usual may become overwhelming if continued attention is not given to board performance and responding to the changing organization or environment.

EXAMINING THE BOARD'S PERFORMANCE

A number of naturally occurring events or organization turning points can stimulate attention to the board's performance. These situations invite the board to consider its own contributions to the organization in ways that do not seem forced or artificial. They include any break in routine or event that interrupts business as usual, such as:

- Loss of a key client or source of revenue;
- Changes in the way a competitor provides some important service or resource;
- Fundamental questions raised by newcomers not familiar with the operating norms. (They ask, "Why do we always do X? Why not try Y?" "What business should we really be in?");
- Decisions that involve competing priorities or forced choices, with tradeoffs that seem (and may really be) irreconcilable;
- Issues of board composition, membership, and retention—a sense that the board does not have the right combination of skills or backgrounds;

- Fundraising pressures—the need to raise capital or launch a campaign or to be more responsive to donors;
- Dissatisfaction and confrontation with key constituents (for example, a labor strike or withdrawal of a major supporter);
- Discovery of a violation of trust—a breach of ethics and morality by someone who represents the organization (for example, embezzlement of funds by an officer);
- Changes in the board's leadership; and
- The resignation (or dismissal) of the chief executive.

Successes also provide occasions for boards to reflect on what happened and how the board contributed to the results. Board members may look beyond mere reaction to external events and consider ways the board might carry out its business more intentionally in the future so as to provide more effective leadership. Whatever the issue, by analyzing its role in the organization's successes or problems, the board can identify lessons that enable it to become more effective in the future.

Even when it is not facing critical turning points, the board can periodically ask its chief executive to talk about some of the major challenges in the coming months. The group can then discuss how it has contributed to the organization's readiness to deal with these matters and how it could prepare itself to provide stronger leadership on them in the future. Thus, the board uses work on substantive challenges to the organization as opportunities to learn how to improve its own performance.

Another opportunity for examination of the board's own performance is in discussions of how the organization is dealing with accountability for its use of resources. Most boards expect the chief executive to report on how staff members are being held accountable, and many boards specify expectations of the chief executive and criteria for assessing that person's performance. Fewer boards, however, apply the same principles to themselves and have clear evidence of how the board itself is being accountable for its use of time and resources.

> **Whatever the issue, by analyzing its role in the organization's successes or problems, the board can identify lessons that enable it to become more effective in the future.**

Developing means for demonstrating the board's own accountability is crucial for modeling the behaviors it expects of others in the organization. Initiating such a process begins with recognizing that the board has a duty of accountability and then engaging in candid discussions of how well it is carrying out this obligation. Useful questions include:

- How is the board itself adding value to the organization?

- What steps should the board take to improve its performance and increase the value it adds to the organization?

- What criteria or indicators will be appropriate for monitoring and demonstrating the board's improved performance?

Intentional examination of the board's commitments and of the ways it will ensure that they are carried out sets the stage for further steps to strengthen individual and group performance. As one experienced board leader advised: "Don't hesitate to ask yourself and others, 'Is this board truly adding as much value to this organization as it could? Could we do better?'" Raising such questions may seem like small beginnings, but numerous boards have found that they are vital first steps toward important changes.

While every member of the board should be concerned about how well the group is doing its job, these concerns must be shared and owned by the full group. The board's leaders are vital to this step, and it usually falls to them to initiate open attention to the board's performance.

The best orchestra or sports team will step back from each performance and review how well it did and where changes could be made to improve future work. As Peter Senge notes in his book *The Fifth Discipline: The Art and Practice of the Learning Organization,* high performing groups take time for practice and for reviewing their performance, thus learning and growing together as a team. Boards can learn from these examples. As the leader of one strong group noted, "After we've finished working a particularly difficult problem, we try to take some time to reflect together on how we can learn from what we've just come through." Boards that take time to examine and reflect upon their own performance together can identify useful lessons that will guide them into increased effectiveness as leaders of their organizations.

ASSESSING PERFORMANCE TO IDENTIFY TARGETS FOR CHANGE

Another way that effective boards apply their skills and add value to the organization is by actively monitoring their own progress and assessing their performance. Most boards are given reams of data on inputs, numbers of clients served, and costs of various programs. Less attention is given to the impacts or results of those activities. Most boards seem unsure about how to measure performance or results of the organization's activities.

Some strong boards have developed sets of specific performance indicators that enable them to monitor performance. These "dashboards" of key

aspects of performance include periodic information on such areas as number of clients served by each program, the costs per contact, numbers of clients completing recommended services, staff assessments of outcomes, and client satisfaction.

Such indicators are especially important as a component of the organization's strategic plan. Each goal in that plan should have accompanying indicators that will allow the board to monitor progress toward its accomplishment. If the plan calls for improvements in the quality of services or staff morale, the board and staff should work together to identify appropriate ways to measure the results of efforts intended to achieve those goals. The results of such efforts provide the board with means to assess progress, to see whether mid-course corrections are needed along the way, and to draw conclusions about the impacts of changes.

> *Boards that take time to examine and reflect upon their own performance together can identify useful lessons that will guide them into increased effectiveness as leaders of their organizations.*

Soliciting input from all participants regarding their views of the board's work, areas warranting attention, and suggestions for change is a step toward improved board performance. As one experienced member emphasized, "Any board interested in improving should get going with an evaluation of its strengths and weaknesses. It should ask a whole series of tough questions about what's working well and what isn't. You can't just depend on a few insiders to run things. You're ALL the owners of the institution and are all responsible for finding ways that enable you to help it work better."

In addition to gathering information for everyone to examine, a crucial function of board assessment is that it spreads responsibility for findings and conclusions across the whole group, thus building consensus for change. In the words of one board chairperson, "The most important result

of starting to evaluate our work as a board was that the group began to think about itself purposively and to ask questions about how we could do our work better in the future. It got us to take responsibility for improving the quality of our own work."

Approaches to board assessment may be divided into two areas: ones that focus on *group* performance and others that address *individual* performance. A few approaches link these domains. Boards can choose among numerous resources—many national associations have developed board assessment tools. Self-assessment approaches include self-evaluations, constituency surveys, third party reviews, internal reviews by an *ad hoc* or standing committee on trusteeship, reflective discussion of critical incidents, and feedback at the conclusion of meetings.

The National Center for Nonprofit Boards offers a comprehensive board self-assessment package. Another approach was developed by the authors, based upon the six competencies of effective boards (for more information see the Resources section on page 16). Other approaches range from brief evaluations at the end of meetings to bringing in outside evaluators to interview and summarize the views of board members, staff, consumers, and sponsors. Each approach has strengths and limitations, so board members are advised to evaluate the available board self-assessment tools and choose the one that best meets their individual needs.

CHARACTERISTICS OF EFFECTIVE BOARDS

Contextual: Effective boards understand and take into account the culture and norms of the organizations they govern. They adapt to the distinctive characteristics and culture of the organization and its staff. They rely on the organization's mission, values, and traditions as guides for their decisions. They act so as to exemplify and reinforce its core values and commitments.

Some of the ways that boards cultivate this competence include:

- Orientations include explicit introduction to the organization's values, norms, and traditions.

- Former members, administrators, and "living legends" are invited to convey the organization's history.

- Current leaders discuss the concepts of shared governance, collegiality, and consensus.

- Leaders review the organization's hallmark characteristics and basic values that set it apart from competitors.

Educational: Effective boards take the necessary steps to ensure that their members are knowledgeable about the organization, the profession, and the board's own roles, responsibilities, and performance. They consciously create opportunities for board education and development and regularly seek information and feedback on the board's own performance. They pause periodically for self-reflection, to assess strengths and limitations, and to examine and learn from the board's mistakes.

Boards learn how to improve their performance through educational programs and retreats, where matters of substance and process are examined. They make use of introspection on the board's internal operations and the ways it carries out business. They reflect on the lessons that can be learned from its own experiences and mistakes.

Some specific ways that boards strengthen this educational competency include:

- Setting aside some time at each meeting for a seminar or workshop to learn about an important matter of substance or process or to discuss a common reading.

- Conducting extended retreats every year or two for similar purposes and for analyzing the board's operations and its mistakes.

- Meeting periodically with "role counterparts" from comparable organizations.

- Rotating committee assignments, so members come to know many aspects of the organization.

- Establishing internal feedback mechanisms such as evaluative comments from members at the end of each meeting, and conducting annual surveys of members on individual and collective performance.

Interpersonal: Effective boards nurture the development of their members as a working group, attend to the board's collective welfare, and foster a sense of cohesiveness. They create a sense of inclusiveness among all members, with equal access to information and equal opportunity to participate and influence decisions. They develop goals for the group, and they recognize group achievements.

Among the ways boards develop this competence are:

- Creating a sense of inclusiveness through events that enable members to become better acquainted with one another, building some "slack time" into the schedule for informal interaction, and sharing information widely and communicating regularly.

- Communicating group norms and standards by pairing newcomers with a mentor or coach.

- Ensuring that the board has strong leadership by systematically grooming its future leaders and encouraging individual skills development.

Analytical: Effective boards recognize the complexities and subtleties of issues and accept ambiguity and uncertainty as healthy preconditions for critical discussions. They approach matters from a broad institutional outlook, and they critically dissect and examine all aspects of multifaceted issues. They raise doubts, explore tradeoffs, and encourage expressions of differences of opinion.

Among the ways that boards cultivate this competence are:

- Analyzing issues and events taking into account multiple potential outcomes and points of view.
- Seeking concrete and even contradictory information on ambiguous matters.
- Asking a few members to be critical evaluators or "devil's advocates," exploring the downside of recommendations.
- Developing contingency and crisis plans.
- Asking members to assume the perspective of key constituencies by role playing.
- Brainstorming alternative views of issues.
- Consulting outsiders and seeking different viewpoints.

Political: Effective boards accept as a primary responsibility the need to develop and maintain healthy relationships among major constituencies. They respect the integrity of the governance process and the legitimate roles and responsibilities of other stakeholders. They consult often and communicate directly with key constituencies, and attempt to minimize conflict and win/lose situations.

Some of the ways that boards nurture this competence include:

- Broadening channels of communication by distributing profiles of board members and annual board reports, inviting staff and consumers to serve on board committees, inviting in outside leaders to address the board, visiting with staff, and establishing multi-constituency task forces.

- Working closely with the chief executive to develop and maintain processes that enable board members to communicate directly with stakeholders.
- Monitoring the health of relationships and morale in the organization.
- Keeping options open and avoiding win/lose polarizations.
- Being sensitive to the legitimate roles and responsibilities of all stakeholders.

Strategic: Effective boards help the organization envision a direction and shape a strategy for the future. They cultivate and concentrate on processes that sharpen organizational priorities. They organize themselves and conduct their business in light of the organization's strategic priorities. They anticipate potential problems and act before issues become crises.

Ways that boards cultivate this competence include:

- Focusing the board's attention on strategic issues by asking the chief executive to present an annual update on organizational priorities and strategy, establishing board priorities and work plans, and developing an annual agenda for the board and its committees.
- Structuring the board's meetings to concentrate on strategic priorities.
- Reinforcing attention to priorities by providing key questions for discussion in advance of meetings, reserving time at each meeting for the chief executive to discuss future issues, and making use of a "consent agenda."
- Developing a board information system that is strategic, normative, selective, and graphic.
- Monitoring the use of board time and attention.

8

RETREATS AS A MEANS TO EXTEND WORK ON BOARD PERFORMANCE

Although we found that board performance is improved most effectively when efforts are integrated into the regular work of the board, retreats are powerful tools for initiating board development efforts and stimulating and extending board strength. A retreat is typically a one to three day special meeting, held off-site and away from wherever the group usually meets. Retreats allow a group to devote extended time to working on a major issue, such as developing or updating its strategic plan, gaining a better understanding of the external environment, clarifying its mission, solving some problem, or many other purposes, including working to improve the board's performance.

A board development retreat is an investment in the future of the board and the organization it governs. A retreat can be a major boost to the board's efforts to make more effective and efficient use of its time. Boards have found that their retreats served a number of important purposes:

- Strengthening performance through a review of governance processes and the board's roles and responsibilities;

- Assessing the board's contributions to the organization and identifying ways it can add greater value;

- Establishing priorities for the board and identifying strategies and actions to achieve them;

- Enhancing collegiality and working relationships among board members and between board and staff; and

- Determining next steps in board development and in the implementation of overall action plans.

Numerous resources are available for boards planning and conducting retreats. The National Center for Nonprofit Boards publishes resource materials on board development and maintains lists of consultants and facilitators. Among the best resources on planning board retreats is Thom Savage's guide, *Seven Steps to a More Effective Board*. A brief primer on planning board retreats is available in Appendix 2 on page 14.

ONGOING BOARD EDUCATION

Incorporating educational activities into board meetings is a vital practice for the ongoing improvement of board's performance. Author Peter Senge observes that boards should be models of "learning organizations." Rather than simply relying on past knowledge and skill, effective boards acknowledge their need to learn and take responsibility for continuing to expand their competencies. They identify topics and issues to examine, develop appropriate programs and resources, and encourage all members to participate in ongoing educational sessions. Special speakers, mini-seminars, study groups, visits with other boards, attendance at conferences on governance, and rotation among committee assignments are among the ways that effective boards encouraged ongoing education.

Thorough orientation programs for incoming members are especially important. New members can get off to a good start if they receive clear expectations for board membership and extensive orientation to the board's roles and responsibilities, as well as information about the organization. Mentoring of each newcomer by a more experienced member is another useful practice that provides both with a greater awareness of board performance. Better boards enlarge this process of education by assisting all members to develop learning plans that will enable them to make greater contributions to the group.

One vital aspect of learning is knowing what information is needed in order to monitor performance. Most boards are familiar with indicators of the organization's financial performance, but few extend their surveillance to other aspects of the organization. Those that do attempt to monitor wider information often find themselves buried in piles of management information, and soon become drawn into second-guessing operational decisions.

Better boards learn what is important to watch and monitor, rather than trying to examine everything. They make use of their strategic plan to identify the specific forms of information they need in order to monitor progress toward key goals and to assess the results of efforts to attain them. These dashboards of key indicators show the organization's progress toward goals.

This process begins with identifying the most critical areas of performance, such as acquisition and allocation of resources as well as utilization, quality, and outcomes of services. Once the board has identified the aspects it wants to monitor, the group identifies the indicators that reveal performance in these areas. Then the board and staff define the desired standards of performance in each of these areas. Finally, it specifies the format and times for receiving all this information. Monitoring them serves to focus the board's attention on those few matters of top priority to its leadership of the organization.

Obtaining and reflecting on feedback about the board's own performance is another vital means for learning. Better boards make assessment of their performance a regular component of the board's responsibility. Getting started with this process can begin with brief assessments at the conclusion of every meeting to obtain participants' views of this session and suggestions to improve the next one. At some point, bringing in outside experts in board performance is important so that the group does not allow blind spots to continue.

RESTRUCTURING MEETING TIME AND COMMITTEE WORK

Another component of improved performance is restructuring the board's use of committees and meeting time to emphasize its strategic priorities. Careful use of the scarce resource of meeting time is a concern of many members. Meeting agendas should be designed so that they sustain focus on key issues of strategy and policy. At the outset, have a member simply monitor the amount of time the board spends on each issue in a meeting and rate its relevance to the board's priorities. The board can consider the relationship between its priorities and its actual use of time.

Better boards limit meeting agendas to a few top priority matters. They cluster routine reports and non-exceptional motions that require board approval into a "consent agenda" that will be voted on in one action rather than separately. Any member can request that an item be separated out for discussion, thus protecting the board's ultimate right to examine any issue. However, the practice allows the board to concentrate its attention on those few matters of highest priority to the organization and avoid getting bogged down in operational details.

Restructuring how the board organizes and charges its committees is another way to improve performance. Instead of committees that mirror management divisions (such as personnel, programs, finances), boards should let form follow function. The strategic priorities provide the point of departure, from which work group assignments and meeting agendas are derived. Board committees should be constructed to focus members' efforts on each of the board's goals, and they should go out of existence when a goal is attained.

How Effective Boards Add Value

The six competencies of effective boards enable the board to add value to the organization by taking actions and reaching decisions that enhance the organization's long-term vitality and quality. Effective boards intentionally cultivate these skills and apply them in a number of ways.

Support the Chief Executive. One basic way effective boards add value to the organization is by helping the chief executive determine what matters most. Working closely with the chief executive, such a board identifies and examines the most significant issues facing the organization and influencing its future. Not every matter is equally important and not all issues can be addressed, so relative priorities must be set. Effective boards concentrate attention on identifying and addressing such matters.

Serve as a Sounding Board. These boards add value by creating opportunities for the chief executive to think aloud about questions and concerns well before it is necessary to come to conclusions or make recommendations. If it is to be of help as a sounding board for the chief executive, candid discussion of embryonic ideas, ambiguous issues, and unclear challenges in the road ahead must be encouraged. Through such unstructured discussions, the board can help the chief executive frame the issue and reflect on the values, alternative directions, and tradeoffs that may eventually lead to a recommendation.

Encourage and Reward Experimentation. Effective boards encourage experimentation, trying out new approaches and alternative ways of dealing with issues. The seeds of change can come from insightful questions that help others "get outside the box" of old assumptions and patterns. Raising critical questions and challenging assumptions stimulate new ideas and creative alternatives for the future of the organization.

Model Effective Behavior. Most importantly, effective boards model the behaviors they desire in others. Boards are appropriately seen as the leaders of the organization, and their decisions are subjected to critical scrutiny by all constituencies. Boards appropriately are concerned about the quality, costs, productivity, and innovation of staff; however, many boards are hesitant to apply the same expectations to themselves. Boards that call for accountability of staff have far greater credibility if they show by example how that is to be done.

Rather than using board meeting time to hear routine reports from every committee, the board can structure its meetings to focus on one or two goals or priorities at each meeting, with discussions led by those groups that have carried out the background preparation.

For changes to outlast individuals and become embedded in the board's culture, there must be some "champions" for the group's performance. In order to build in advocacy for the board itself, members can assign to a group the task of keeping the board reminded of its commitments, monitoring its performance, and periodically recommending actions that will strengthen meeting processes. Better boards have the nominating committee or some other permanent group take responsibility for developing and implementing steps for monitoring board meetings, soliciting participants' assessments and recommendations for improvement, and arranging for periodic board education sessions and retreats on issues of interest.

Many boards expand the duties of the nominating committee to include carrying out periodic assessments of individual and group performance. They use these findings to coach members in expanding their leadership contributions to the board, to identify persons to nominate for additional terms, to identify skills needed in new members, and to plan regular educational sessions in areas the board needed improvement.

It broadens the scope of characteristics sought in new members to include skills in working with groups, linkages to key constituencies, ability to contribute new perspectives to examining issues, and a track record of making positive contributions to group communication and learning.

Boards that restructure their meeting agendas and committees then monitor the usefulness of those changes through evaluation. Brief assessment forms, followed by discussion of participants' concerns and recommendations, can lead to more productive and satisfying meetings.

BUILDING GROUP COHESION AND TEAMWORK

For most board members, structural changes are more attractive than efforts directed explicitly at relationships, processes, or communications. However, the most effective boards took careful steps to transform an assembly of talented individuals into a well integrated group.

Many board members are comfortable providing individual expertise or advice to the chief executive, while others see their service taking place on a committee related to their area of interest. The most effective boards went beyond these efforts and also emphasized the group as the decision-making unit. A cohesive board makes better decisions than do individuals, while drawing upon members' multiple perspectives to avoid the traps of "groupthink."

Transforming an assembly of skilled individuals into a well integrated team is a long and difficult process. It requires taking critical issues to the group for deliberation and taking the time necessary to hear the views of each participant. It requires that the issues taken to the board are vital to the future of the organization, not window dressing. It requires making sure that everyone has equal access to information. It requires taking time for members to get to know one another beyond the formal setting of the boardroom.

Better boards pay careful attention to communications among members, to nurturing and sustaining inclusive relationships and a sense of mutual responsibility for the board's success. They are aware that the silent member may have some important concerns that the board needs to hear.

Working to formulate goals for the board itself is a good means for building group cohesion while also serving to focus the board's use of time and energy. Goals for the board itself should be distinct from but lead to the organization's overall goals. Board goals identify specifically what the board will do in order to maximize its contributions to the attainment of the organization's goals.

Board goals should be posted in conspicuous places and repeated in meetings and reports. Keeping the board goals paramount in meetings by means of the agenda plan and the focus of each report or discussion keeps everyone clear about the purpose and direction of each step. It also allows the board to monitor and evaluate its own progress toward its goals.

Formulating specific goals for the board also helps the process of clarifying expectations of the board as a group. It is important to make sure that each participant understands what is expected of him or her as well has how those expectations contribute to overall goals. Setting goals for the board as a whole and periodically reviewing progress toward them serve to maintain the board's attention to its own performance and how it adds value to the organization.

Throughout these steps, an underlying issue is developing a stronger sense of inclusiveness and cohesiveness among board members as a group. This requires paying careful attention to communications among members and intentionally nurturing and sustaining inclusive relationships. These processes should begin at recruitment and orientation, be carried forward by all leaders, and reinforced at social times and retreats.

CONCLUSION

By working intentionally on its own performance, a board fundamentally changes the ways it uses time and energy, rather than merely applying a quick fix to an immediate problem. Attention to how it is carrying out its work becomes part of the agenda, rather than something separate from ongoing tasks and responsibilities. Effective board development includes incorporating into its basic sense of responsibility a continuing concern with improving performance, rather than seeing it as something separate or occasional.

Leaders can reinforce this understanding by pausing occasionally during discussions or at the conclusion of a major agenda item to invite reflection on *how* the group dealt with the issue and what could be done to improve the process next time. Such reflective practices become part of the group's culture.

Taking time for reflection on how the board has used its time and attention, particularly after dealing with a difficult issue, enhances the group's ownership of its processes and performance. Such discussions should take place at the conclusion of each meeting and allow members to share perceptions of performance and consider ways to improve future meetings.

In conclusion, effective boards attend to *how* they work together as well as to *what* they do. Members take responsibility for initiating discussions of ways the group carries out its work and seek ways to improve performance. They take advantage of breaks or turning points in the organization's experience to draw attention to the board's role in leadership and change. They test out their perceptions with others and identify shared concerns of the group. They move ahead by means of assessments of group performance to identify specific issues and goals for change. They lay the foundation for on-going work by means of retreats and careful follow-up. They reinforce and institutionalize changes by means of in-meeting discussions of feedback on performance and educational sessions that contribute to strengthening the board's effectiveness.

These efforts bridge the gap between learning and doing, integrating reflection with work. They help the group to develop a culture of active responsibility for making ongoing, self-directed improvements in its own performance. By taking consistent initiatives to improve their work together, boards set the example for others and show how to add greater value to their organizations. ■

Appendix 1

Demonstration Project on Improving Board Performance: The Methodology

With support from the Lilly Endowment and the Kellogg Foundation, Dick Chait, Barbara Taylor, and I undertook a five-year study of board development, examining the impacts of purposive efforts to increase ordinary boards' skills in the six competency areas discussed earlier. Eleven organizations were selected from a large pool of volunteers. The study included six small private liberal arts colleges, two hospitals (one large, the other small), two social service organizations, and one large public university. For each of these sites, we recruited a matched counterpart to allow for comparisons between boards receiving intervention and those without.

We measured each board's current performance through members' self-ratings and individual interviews. These assessments were taken at the beginning of the project and again at the conclusion of the training period, thus allowing for documentation of changes in the boards receiving the coaching and comparisons with those not receiving the interventions. We also collected information on key aspects of the finances of these organizations over the time of the project in order to examine possible linkages between board performance and organizational performance.

The next phase of the project began with retreats for each board, followed by individualized consultation and coaching at subsequent board meetings at each site. The steering committee that each board appointed to work with project staff planned a retreat for its full board. While the details varied among boards, the retreats lasted about a day and a half. They were informal and separate from formal board meetings.

Through case studies and small group work sessions, board members explored board competencies and developed a tailored plan to strengthen weak skills while working on the board's substantive priorities. The action plan developed by each board identified areas and skills that needed its attention.

Most boards elected to focus considerable attention on the educational competency, seeking to ensure that members became better informed about the organization and the board's roles, responsibilities, and performance. Project staff provided consultation regarding various methods and approaches to use in strengthening performance, while the board as a group decided how to proceed with its work.

Project staff also provided ongoing consultation and coaching on a wide variety of board activities. In short, the project provided facilitation, coaching, and consultation while the boards worked on their substantive concerns. The emphasis was on how effectively the board addressed its concerns and carried out its governance responsibilities. Strengthening board processes and skills for dealing with its current issues was believed to provide a generalizable base for addressing future concerns more effectively. Throughout these efforts, a key objective was to incorporate clear norms and effective processes directly into the board culture so they became routine components of its operating style.

Performance in the six competencies was measured again at the conclusion of the study, and comparisons made with those taken at the outset.

The Findings

The findings indicated extensive improvements and benefits for the overall performance of those boards receiving the coaching. The members noted the most extensive gains in the educational area, while the interview approach found gains in the contextual, interpersonal, and analytic competencies as well. The interview approach revealed major changes over time at the intervention sites, while the self-assessments indicated major differences in performance between those sites that had received the interventions and those that had not.

A comparison of financial performance between those organizations receiving the interventions and those not receiving them showed markedly greater gains for intervention sites in most areas compared to those that did not receive intervention. Those boards that received coaching demonstrated significant improvements in their performance over the course of the project, and the organizations they led also made markedly greater gains than did their matched counterparts. The project demonstrated the multiple positive impacts of board development efforts. ∎

Appendix 2

Steps in Planning a Board Retreat

Retreats provide an opportunity for the board to take an in-depth look at its performance. For a retreat to be successful, it should begin with a broad agreement among board members, concerning:

- The purposes and expectations of the retreat;
- The board's perceived needs;
- Possible topics to be covered and the approach to each; and
- The allocation of responsibilities and tasks for implementation.

Outside facilitators who are skilled in board development can bring new ideas and comparative perspectives to issues a board is facing. Facilitators can moderate discussions and encourage participation, raise provocative questions more easily than insiders, press the group to clarify and address conflicts, assist them in reaching conclusions, and help to identify concrete action steps. "Our facilitator really stirred the pot, asked tough questions and encouraged us to do the same thing and not back off," said one respondent. The neutrality of an outside facilitator enables participants to separate ideas or proposals from the source and thus avoid the impediments of old disagreements.

The board chairperson and the chief executive of the organization carry vital leadership roles in developing plans for the retreat. They should work with a representative group of board leaders to identify issues to be addressed and to formulate an agenda. The committee should also identify a facilitator to help plan the program and format. The plan and agenda would then be circulated in draft form among the board for comment and revision.

The planning committee may carry out an assessment of the current performance and practices of the board, making use of one or more of the approaches described previously.

This evaluation process may include consideration of many aspects of the board's work, such as:

- The leadership provided by the chairperson, chief executive, and committee chairs;
- The board's committee structure and meeting processes;
- Members' understanding of their roles and responsibilities;
- Present and future needs of the organization;
- Use of meeting time and members' skills;
- Communication patterns among board members;
- Relationships with key constituencies and their influences upon the board's governance processes;
- The board's values, members' understanding of organizational mission and environmental trends;
- How well the board provides guidance to the chief executive and senior staff, how it monitors their performance and provides feedback; and
- The financial condition of the organization and how the board is dealing with this area.

Such assessments can help the committee identify areas of shared concern that warrant attention. Likewise, the process will show how ready the members are to learn and work together.

The retreat agenda should be designed to address the shared concerns of board members. The agenda should not be overcrowded or overtaxing to participants, nor should it involve lengthy reports or speeches. The emphasis is on wide-ranging discussion, not on business as usual. Time for participants to reflect on issues together and to enjoy one another's company are crucial.

Retreat Format

Once the board commits itself to having a retreat, the planning committee develops the agenda and oversees local arrangements at the site.

After beginning the retreat with a summary of the main issues or questions on which work is to be focused, many boards have found it very productive to break into smaller groups for more intensive examination of specific parts of them. These discussions should be guided by concrete, action-oriented questions or tasks developed by the planning committee prior to the retreat and modified as needed during the retreat.

Working on such questions or tasks in small groups, rather than with the whole board, stimulates much greater participation by creating safer environments for people to share ideas and explore new directions.

The emphasis should be on full participation in open explorations of issues and alternative responses. Moderators of small group discussions should take care to encourage those who have not spoken to share their impressions and ideas. Those who have served on other boards should be invited to compare their experiences and offer suggestions for alternative approaches to issues.

Each group session should result in a brief oral summary and a written set of recommendations that it then presents to the full board. After the full board has heard and discussed the reports of all groups, it works on overall conclusions and priorities among them. Then it develops an explicit action plan for implementation of decisions following the retreat. It identifies its priorities among the recommendations and then allocates specific responsibilities for action to individuals and task forces.

In order to prepare to monitor progress on its conclusions, the board should determine what evidence will serve to indicate movement or progress on each goal. Some examples of indicators of progress that boards have developed include:

- Greater attendance at board meetings;

- More useful, concise, and directed committee reports;

- Clearer sense of mission and purpose among members;

- Better informed and prepared members;

- Improved agendas, with high priority issues given prime attention;

- Greater sense of trust and inclusiveness among members;

- Regular self-evaluations by board;

- Increased giving and getting by members; and

- Explicit orientation program for every new member.

The selection of indicators of board progress should be based upon the specific areas identified by the board as its targets for the coming year.

At the conclusion of the retreat, assess the experience and highlight major conclusions. Possibly go around the room and have each participant share a final thought, hope, concern, or lesson from the retreat. This reinforces the principle of equal participation and allows each person to bring some closure to the experience. The group should also specify how it will share its conclusions with any members who were unable to be present. Finally, the chairperson or the chief executive outlines the next steps the board will take in the weeks ahead.

Immediately after the retreat, the committee and facilitator should meet to assess the conclusions and agree on a division of labor. Leaders should incorporate into the next meeting at least one or two ideas that emerged directly from the retreat. This serves to build momentum and underscore the utility of the retreat.

The committee should then prepare a written report that summarizes the findings of each group session and the overall recommendations and specific action steps to be taken over the coming months. The report should clearly identify who is responsible for following up on the implementation of each conclusion from the retreat. It should be brought to the next regular meeting of the board for formal adoption into action plans.

A retreat can generate a great deal of enthusiasm; however, a board can lose momentum when it returns to its regular meeting schedule. Explicit methods for reminding everyone of the agreements and changes identified at the retreat and regular evidence of how those resolutions are being implemented are essential. The underlying goal is to build habits of reflection and learning into the group's culture, so newcomers (as well as old-timers) are socialized into effective patterns of behavior. ■

Suggested Resources

Association for Governing Boards of Universities and Colleges. *Self-Study Criteria for Governing Boards of Independent Colleges and Universities.* Washington, DC: 1986.

Practical tools for assessing the performance of boards of education organizations.

Carver, John. *Boards That Make a Difference: A New Design for Leadership in Nonprofit and Public Organizations.* San Francisco: Jossey-Bass, 1990, 242 pages.

Thoughtful advice from an experienced consultant to many boards.

Chait, Richard, Thomas Holland, and Barbara Taylor. *The Effective Board of Trustees.* Phoenix: Oryx Press, 1993, 140 pages.

This volume describes the distinguishing characteristics of highly effective boards and examines their practices in developing those skills.

Chait, Richard, Thomas Holland, and Barbara Taylor. *Improving the Performance of Governing Boards.* Phoenix: Oryx Press, 1996.

This volume from the ACE/Oryx Press Series on Higher Education builds on the authors' previous book and discusses a range of practical steps boards can take to make continuous improvements part of their work.

Chait, Richard. *The New Activism of Corporate Boards and the Implications for Campus Governance.* Washington, DC: Association of Governing Boards of Universities and Colleges, 1994.

This book suggests that changes in corporate board members' expectations will bring about greater demands on college presidents and trustees.

Drucker, Peter. "Lessons for Successful Nonprofit Governance." *Nonprofit Management and Leadership,* Vol. 1, No. 1, 1990, pp. 7-14.

This essay sets forth several key guidelines for boards, from the senior leader of the field.

Fry, Ronald E. "Accountability in Organizational Life: Problem or Opportunity for Nonprofits?" *Nonprofit Management and Leadership,* Vol. 6, No. 2, 1995, pp 181-195.

This thoughtful essay provides a positive and constructive approach to mutual accountability on boards.

Herman, Robert D. & Van Til, J. *Nonprofit Boards of Directors: Analyses and Applications.* New Brunswick, N.J.: Transaction Publishers, 1989.

This volume summarizes recent research on boards and discusses implications for trustees.

Holland, Thomas. "Self-Assessment by Nonprofit Boards." *Nonprofit Management and Leadership,* Vol. 2, No. 1, 1991, pp. 25-36.

This article describes the development and testing of a tool for assessing board performance.

Holland, Thomas. "Culture and Change in Nonprofit Boards." *Nonprofit Management and Leadership,* Vol. 4, No. 2, 1993, pp. 141-155.

This article says that changes in the underlying norms and expectations of board members are essential for improvements in performance.

Holland, Thomas, Richard Chait, and Barbara Taylor. "Board Effectiveness: Identifying and Measuring Trustee Competencies." *Journal of Research in Higher Education,* Vol. 30, No. 4, 1989, pp. 451-469.

This article describes the original research that identified the six sets of characteristics of highly effective boards.

Houle, Cyril O. *Governing Boards: Their Nature and Nurture.* San Francisco: Jossey Bass, 1989, 223 pages.

This booklet offers wise advice from a seasoned observer and consultant to many boards.

Pound, J. "The Promise of the Governed Corporation." *Harvard Business Review,* March-April 1993, pp. 89-98.

This article says that moving from watchdog to partner is crucial for effective relationships between boards and their chief executives.

Savage, Thomas J. *Seven Steps to a More Effective Board.* Rockville, MD: The Cheswick Center, 1994, 100 pages.

A practical guide to conducting successful retreats for board development.

Senge, Peter. *The Fifth Discipline: The Art and Practice of the Learning Organization.* New York: Doubleday, 1994.

Becoming a team that learns to improve by reflecting on its own performance is essential for a strong organization. This important volume describes how organizations develop skills of learning.

Schein, E. H. "How Can Organizations Learn Faster? The Challenge of Entering the Green Room." *Sloan Management Review,* Winter 1993, pp. 85-92.

Learning new skills involves anxiety and hope for greater effectiveness. Leaders must balance these forces for groups to learn.

Slesinger, Larry. *Self-Assessment for Nonprofit Governing Boards.* Washington, DC: National Center for Nonprofit Boards, 1995, 60 pages.

A practical set of tools for use by any board that wants to assess its performance and identify areas needing improvement.

Smith, D. H. *Entrusted: The Moral Responsibilities of Trusteeship.* Bloomington: Indiana University Press, 1995.

Thoughtful reflections on the basic duties of board members and the values underlying them.

Zander, Alvin. *Making Boards Effective: The Dynamics of Governing Boards.* San Francisco: Jossey-Bass, 1993, 169 pages.

This volume examines the group process of boards and how interpersonal relationships influence their performance.